Swans to Carry Me

Earl Vincent de Berge

Cyberwit.net
HIG 45 Kaushambi Kunj, Kalindipuram
Allahabad - 211011 (U.P.) India
http://www.cyberwit.net
Tel: +(91) 9415091004
E-mail: info@cyberwit.net

Printed at QUARTERFOLD PRINTABILITIES.

PREFACE AND ACKNOWLEDGEMENTS

SWANS TO CARRY ME

(donkeys, dogs, lizards and sheep too)

This volume is divided into two main sections. The first presents some of my reflections on environment, society, aging, religion, time and peace of mind. In the second section my focus is on the animal world which has enriched my life for eight decades. My wife and I chose to live in the wonderful wild environments of Arizona and northern Mexico as well as sustained diversions in Central America. During these years I was lucky to have the time and resources to try my hand at several forms of self-expression: poetry, photography, essay writing, metal sculpture and even farming. I discovered that I am too lazy to master any aspect of music, except listening to those many who have. Unfortunately, I also neglected learning about the arts of cooking, singing, acting, and dancing. But poetry, short stories and photography proved to be fine challenges. I greatly enjoyed abstract metal sculpture, but gave it up at age 70 because welding gases made me sick.

In this second selection of poems from my writings spanning 1959 to 2022, I continue to celebrate my journey through life with honest people, with pets, farm and in-the-wild animals, coupled with musings about time, environment, over-population, the universe, and theories of God as expressed in western religions. I am neither an atheist nor a believer. I have found no logical reason to accept or reject the hypothesis that a God created the clockwork that is the universe. Visionaries who advanced moral teaching of great value impress me: Jesus, Plato, Buddha, Confucius, Navajo and Maya "seers."

I have included several of my photographs and photo abstractions in this volume.

Although trained as a political scientist and public opinion researcher, I try to avoid publishing much about politics, except for an occasional outburst in social media, because most contemporary politicians seem too self-impressed to achieve intellectual or behavioral honesty. And their greed for power is simply breathtaking. The latest crop includes madmen such as Putin, Trump and Kim Jong-un, and cyphers such as Ted Cruz. Politicians have become a key reason I prefer to focus my attention on nature and the lives of plain folk.

Several individuals have been important in encouraging me to write prose, essays and poetry, including Mark Winheld, P.J. Erickson, Russell Avery, Cynthia Hogue, Terrance Bracy, John Gabusi, Jim Haynes, Diane Christensen, Linda de Berge Firestone, Steve Tuttle, and Suzanne, my bride of six decades. And at Antioch College, I learned that if people can't fathom the meaning of my words, as I mean them, it is my fault.

Special thanks to Dr. Karunesh Kumar Agrawal at Taj Mahal Review for taking an interest in my poetical efforts and producing this book.

Earl Vincent de Berge 2022

Contents

Observations & Reflections

SWANS TO CARRY ME

Breath of spring is everywhere
        in every face and flower,
its smiles and scents beguile.
        I dream of swans that carry me
to where I've never been before.

1996

DON CHINTO AT 80

Skilled with shovel and hoe
in his hands so many years
– his fingers curve to each tool
like an ancient vine to an enduring tree.
Their handles as polished as fine furniture,
his sons will use them at his burial.

2010
Chocolá, Guatemala

FROM BOTH HANDS

From her strong deliberate fingers
forged by cherished work of weaving,
flows the culturally schooled and skilled touch
of a master craftsman sure of her work
and purposefully adding her own variations.

From her left hand streams her view of
traditional cultural design. From her right
comes power and precision. Together she
creates a living art. Watching her hands is like
seeing and hearing a Bach fugue unfold.

2018
Watching a weaver in Xela, Guatemala

HUMILIATION

The humiliation of a people is seen
in the streets of a farm trading town
as a Maya family shoulders the coffin
of an infant toward the humblest level
of the community burial grounds.

Behind the mourning bearers, three
non-Maya teens taunt and wickedly throw
stones at their grief-slumped backs.

The cortége continues, silently shuffling
down the hill and into their metaphysical
world as would be their choice - even had
Europeans and their racism never come.

1999
Chichicastenango, Guatemala

ENCHANTMENT LOST

Far from the urban pulse,
night sweetly fashions islands
of darkness and clear views
of the sea of stars puncturing
flawless black silk.

But a time creeps upon our necks
when few in the developed world
will witness the mystic Milky Way
or our galaxy's errant planets
gracefully easing westward.

All our night firmaments will
become canopies of reflected
light as Earth glows with squander.
This cannot be what God meant by:
"And let there be light."

2008 Navajo Reservation

SPINNING IN EMPTINESS

Alone in the emptiness of time
spinning toward where we have never
been, we arrive at moments without end
in a time and place not long a home.

Where did time come from — where is it going?
When is a moment unique to itself,
when the end of every moment is imperceptible
from the dawn and the dusk of the next?

I think, therefore I am.
I cease thinking, therefore I am not.
Clear, simple, all that I need.

The stone eyelid of time blinks at nothing.
I face whatever is next, unafraid and
with my mind focused on perfection
of balance, tolerance and kindness.

2006

ARISTOTLE ARGUES

Aristotle argues that human flourishing
requires philosophizing quietly pursuing
truth for its intrinsic quality.

Seneca had similar lofty visions for leisure time,
writing: "I am not sure that we cannot serve
the Commonwealth better when we are at
leisure to inquire into what virtue is."

Trump asks "Who are these jokers?"

2019

ETERNAL SEA AWAITS

The eternal sea awaits,
        enchanting and calm,
a yearning mistress longing,
        yet confident her ephemeral
lover will sweep into her arms
        as a great gale, stirring her depths
to foaming passion until they both
        climax on the rocks and subside
to lie docile in one another's arms.
        He caresses her with a gentle breeze,
 waiting to regain their passion.

2021

ASCENDING DESCENT

My descent into later
   years
has been a happy
   ascent
into freedom of thought
   unfettered
by tasks I once
   valued.
Each day is now
   renewal
and wonder at all the
   details
I was too busy to notice
   in youth.

2015

ASPEN AT PRAYER

A cluster of quaking aspen stand
white skin naked in winter's breeze.
Once golden leaves are scattered all around.
Bare, silent up-reaching branches make no sound
yet their slender fingers rising into winter air
seem to be making this small prayer:
Oh, winter haze and cold, please fade soon
bring back the warmth of sun each noon

2021

ATOP A BOXCAR

Dad was born under the same
wandering star the old drunk character
in Cat Ballou sang about. And it hovered
above me when as a teen Dad wandered
North America with my sister and me in tow.

He loved trains from his teenage
days when he fled his boozing father
and jumped boxcars headed South
or West – where they ran, he went.

And where his wanderlust went –
    train museums
    train crossings
    rail yards
    round houses
    ding-ding crossings
    trestles everywhere
    lonely stretches
    abandoned tracks ...
 we went.

With him America became a part of me:
   ... camping in its agitated shadows,
   ... quaking motel rooms near the tracks,
   ... trailer windows open to awaken a memory
    and plant one in me
   ... on hillsides watching, listening
   ... all his homes were within ear-shot

of their whistles
... new engines come to town — we were there
startled by steam exhausts
... stink from their stacks
he, then I, loved it all.

When diesels took over
he headed to Old Mexico
where old U.S. steam locomotives flourished,

Trains and drifters powered his soul —
with an ear to a main-line rail,
he told me how hobos gauged
a train's distance and made their plans
... how they used a train's immense weight
to forge knives and spoons from nails,
and how I could make shiny charms
for my sister from pennies.
He told me one day how a train squashed
his wedding ring into useful metal.

He bought me electric toy trains of the
Atchison, Topeka and the Santa Fe.

Arms outstretched for balance we would stride
on rails, across trestles, collect train artifacts.
Wave at the engineer and men in the caboose –
they had cabooses in the old days.

Double track lines were favorites
clickety-clack became a four/four rhythm
urging him to move on and not look back.

I still love trains and imagine Dad
sitting cross-legged atop a boxcar
in his 20s – shirt whipping in the wind.

2009

BEFORE TIME

Before time was calculated
in earnest by troublemakers
who couldn't leave well-enough alone,
mankind had fewer ulcers.

Being "on time" was silly
because doing so would not
earn you anything and besides
you'd be the only one there.

Seasons were simply
changes in temperature,
migratory birds showing up –
no flower was named Four O'clock.

2013

IN THE MOUTH OF NIGHT

Lying unalone, yet alone in
the closed mouth of night,
the patrolman's whistle says

"all is well" in the moonless
darkness. Silence descends,
settles against my skin.

She stirs in a dream as
somewhere deep in the house
a door creaks in a breath of air.

Memories bloom in my mind
of youthful nights lying on desert's
floor, unaware of loneliness.

2007 Quito

TODAY OR TOMORROW?

Would the gentlemen like their coffee
        today or tomorrow?
asked the waiter with a grin that showed
        a missing front tooth,
the result, perhaps of asking other gents
        the same question.
I said *Today would be fine*
        and if what you bring is hot,
I will consider leaving a tip
        today or tomorrow.
Same toothless smile spreads
        but the coffee materializes
this time with the words:
        "It's on the house ...
tomorrow, not today!"

1962
Guerero Negro, Mexico

FIELD AND STREAM MAGAZINE

"A Hunter Was Here" boasts the tag line
beside a cover photo of a fresh bloody hand print
slapped on white Aspen as hunter in head-to-toe
camouflage walks away nonchalantly
through winter's snow with deer head
strapped to his ergonomic backpack.
"Only another hunter would appreciate
my marking of the tree in this way"
the magazine claims the hunter said.
— No one interviewed the deer.

Hey big shot hunter with scoped rifle,
thermal underwear, camouflage, water-
proof boots, energy-rich food packs,
warm gloves and music in your ear-buds.
You've come a long way in your 4 by 4
from the days when cavemen risked
their lives for food from bison and bears
before leaving hand images near
cave drawings of beasts they killed
with spears in hand-to-claw combat.

2014

A LITTLE MOZART AND . . .

It must be Summer – the sun breaks
        the horizon before I rise.

Our lambs have stopped bawling –
        their noses dropped into tall grass.

Could be Fall, if it weren't so hot –
        only shade trees offer relief.

No, it is Summer – cacti are in bloom
        and our citrus are plump with juice.

I'm getting older: some joints ache
        and younger men trim our tall trees,

clean ditches and fix what needs fixing.
        But my dogs still seek my hand.

Music and books dream with me
        and I still pursue rebellious thoughts

as I pursue goals that are worth a darn
        and with a little Mozart, I'm just fine.

2013

BETTER COMPANIONS

We are born innocent and alone
to later die alone less than innocent.
Why waste time lamenting mortality when
so much beautiful opportunity lies in life.

Between the bookends of life, celebrate
the grace and scent of flowers, gifts of speech,
inventive minds, the smiling faces of love calling us
to consider how to understand and best achieve grace.

But between the bookends so many are slaves
to the pursuit of power, casting suspicion on others
and building more efficient ways for killing or hating
strangers – who in turn, learn to return the favor.

We will each be alone at the end. Why persist in
the pursuit of hate and power when love and sharing
are such better companions with which to travel?

2007

AROLDO LANDSCAPING

Before dawn, his cared-for pickup
is loaded as he and two countrymen
leave South Phoenix for Scottsdale.

Rakes, brooms, blowers, chain saws,
shovels, hoes, fertilizers, trash bags
hedge clippers, long-pole limb saws.

Happy to work as self-owned slaves
for rich companies that are amused to pay
him a cut rate to tidy office grounds

while inside the office, Aroldo's client signs
checks for candidates to build a border wall
to keep Aroldo's refugee workers out.

Aroldo looks up at the head man's window
for a clue on the meaning of words
shouted his way: *cut-o that branch-o!*

Aroldo is a naturalized citizen and his wife
has work papers. Minding their business,
they work like ghosts in American shadows.

2017

CLIMATE CHANGE

What we gonna do
when the wells run dry,
the oceans rise and
forests burn or die?

Cultures evolved in rhythms
to when the sun's angle
said it was time to plant
or migrate south like geese.

North folk made no fuss
when it got hot or cold
as the sun skittered predictably
in the heavens of clean air.

At the Andean equator spring
was eternal in the mountains and
summer perpetual on the beaches.
Will our next future always be hot?

What we gonna do
when we need a new God
to explain why there ain't no food
and the sky is raining ash?

2013 Peru

DEATH WITHOUT HONOR

Death without pursuit of honor
is the norm for most of us —
our lives aimed at family, food and housing
and at getting along, minding our own
business and not seeking laurels.

Death with honor?
And the winners are...

2013

DESTINY

Human destiny is not predetermined
by nature's laws or a clockwork
of Newtonian physics any more
than by the handiwork of a god
overseeing a moral trial that moves
monotonously while making judgments.
Nor is destiny a random series of events
amounting to little more than chaos.

Your destiny is a montage of vectors and
fortuity spiced with your free will to make
judgements of what is good and bad.
Destiny is immersed in the swirling madness
of life constrained only by the totality of
physics and time – so complex that feeling
confused is natural to sentient beings.

To cope, we invent meaning in everything
lest we be forced to come to grips
with the fearful reality that nothing lasts
except metamorphosis and the interaction
of kaleidoscopic forces without motive.

As man is the master of himself
so must he control his thoughts
and resist being driven by theories
of the unknowable conjured by shepherds.

2004

CHILD AT THE BORDER

I am small and alone
             huddled before
badges, uniforms
             and the red faces
of Americans
             shaking fists,
mouthing curses
             I cannot understand.

I wither beneath
             their anger.
Does my fear not give
             them pause?
Will I see my mother
             ever again?

I am a tragedy
             small and alone
                  I wither.

2014
Nogales, Az

DIVIDED CORE

My core was divided in youth
        and remains so.
I loved cities, their art, music
        constant change
and so many people in modes of
        crisis and creativity.

But as well, what a joy it was
        to be immersed in a wilderness,
a living essence free of motive,
        filled with worlds of tranquil beauty,
rewarding and punishing nothing –
        for wilderness simply is.

To neither can I now commit
        for my aging marrow
seeks solitude from the
        harnesses of action
— ever pulling me toward
        meditation.

2010

INSIDE MY LONG COAT

Inside my long coat of memories
    float fragrances of youth
tugging my heart to set aside
    tasks that might be done.
Small memories from the desert
    trail that eddy.
Pockets, so personal,
    amazing what they hold!

The perfumes of
    Stout old leather that
        creaks with comforting sighs.
    Cleaning solvent and oil
        on shotguns after hunting.
    Flowering cactus somewhere
        out of sight.
    A campfire and dying embers
        beneath the mouth of stars.
    Pancakes, bacon and toast
        at dawn.
    Creosote bush scents heralding
        the prospect of rain.
    Clean socks and dry boots
        before we hit the trail.
    Sounds of men suiting up
        for a day of adventure.

2008

ASK ANY ANT

Ego makes the heart
            grow fonder of itself.
One must age to realize
            that civilization
cares not that you exist unless ...
            you owe taxes,
            are late on payments,
            commit a nasty crime
            are broke, are rich
            or have big breasts.
Civilization has no expectation you will
            become a wonder of any kind ...
            but if you do, will try to steal
            some gravy from your plate.
Civilization does not give a damn
            whether you step into the room
            with a bright idea or are just looking
            for an unoccupied outhouse.
Civilization briefly rewards strength
            determination and loyalty,
            all unremarkably common traits.

Ask any ant.

2014

THREE LIVES

BLUE BOY
An unusually small Guatemalan lad
of 12 or 13 years clothed in blue begins
each day with his body and brain devoted
to finding work and buying food to give him
enough energy to get up each tomorrow
to search for more shoes to shine and food.

BLACK BOY
Blue boy has long been an icon to me
of how poverty wastes youthful potential.
This morning I saw an even younger
boy in torn black rags from head to toe,
crawling among the legs of tourists.
He pushed a dinged-up donation cup
before him on the scuffed concrete.
A park policeman in no uncertain terms
ushered him out of the view of tourists.

WHITE GIRL
Born albino, the weak-eyed Maya girl
and her mother were quickly abandoned.
"She is a sign of the devil and the fault
lies with the mother!" the father bawled
and left to fortify his decision in a bottle.

Since a toddler, the white girl and mom
sell tourist trinkets in the park and now
as a young adult, she does so still.

Each night she sleeps with all her goods
in plastic bags in a doorway across from the
police precinct station arched entrance.
She rarely looks up.

2013 Antigua

EXTINCTION

Mankind mushrooms in number while laughing
from the perfidious view that annihilation
of other species can never include our own.

Meanwhile, under relentless population growth
basic human demands become dominant,
open spaces succumb to slums and innocuous
microbes and viruses become pandemic.

Exploration for new frontiers is exhausted,
stalls to a hapless search for privacy and safety.
Virgin soils and waterways become toxic dumps,
genetic engineering replaces diversity
— the ultimate undoing of survival through evolution.

Once ubiquitous wilderness becomes myth,
as mankind, seeking food, water and shelter
grasps greedily at all it must possess
like ants stripping a weakened spider in its web.

Our craving to multiply assures
mankind the extinction of others –
doves, whales, elephants, snails.
Our growth is their disaster.

It is also becoming our own.

2013

TIME AND LIGHT

As last sunlight retreats up valley slopes
its rays, like time, slide into oblivion.

In the morning, sunlight will race in renewal
down the slopes until it fills every dark valley.

Time is ever voting and painting with light
never waiting, never yawning, never bored.

Light and time make a billion stops per second
yet never rest in their pursuit of everything.

The essence of both is that they never pause.

2015

WHILE AMERICA DIVIDES

We are not what we were,
cannot be, should not strive to be.
We were never what romantics
claimed we were. They ever made
our identity mythical and heroic
make-believe: John Wayne, Mae West
Groucho Marx, Tom Sawyer,
the Cisco Kid, Louis Armstrong
Meryl Streep and Tom Hanks.

America's history is awash in conflict:
civil war, Indian wars, states' rights,
great and small depressions
Blacks under the heel of Whites
Asians and Latins the same
and now, Whites feeling the heels
of Whites, Blacks, Mexicans and Asians ...
every darn one of us — heeling or heeled.

But we can change —
help citizens and aspirants feel pride,
give texture and meaning to liberty
glorify what is clean, natural and good.
America the beautiful, the brave, and
the melting pot of cherished diversity.

We must not long to return to illusions
that were created to rewrite American
history as a romantic, fairyland of peace,

bravery and equity in laws. Cultural sanity
demands we face what we are, search for
what is better, richer, more honest ...
become what we can become, fully
embrace again diversity's power.
Kindle the vitality of unity and respect.

2013

WHO DECIDED?

If God made Earth,
upon which the male
and female of every species
are having sex whenever
and wherever they can ...
who decided sex is a sin?

And just as Jesus
turned water into wine
so do men turn grapes into wine
and wine into poetry and music.
Some folk must be gods.

2014

FACEBOOK THE HERALD

Daily herald of impotence where,
in isolation, millions tender applause, hopes,
anger, despair, fear and pain in streams
of triumph or release. Solitary individuals
sharing intimacies of their views with anyone
who will "like" or offer sympathetic caresses
... "U R not alone"

It is a herald for love givers and seekers
who float in its metaphysical ether,
keeping intimacy at a distance
while laying themselves naked
to the smirks of gawkers.

Facebook, herald of dogmatic anger ...
"I think like this and I'm right.
Screw you if you don't like it."
(unsaid: thank God you read this -
I have no one to yell at but my TV.)

Facebook, the moon face of love given or sought,
a coffin for anger and despair, a stage for shouting
"Up yours" — "I'm sorry!"

2013

DO GOOD NOW

Join me to witness cactus flowering
brilliantly in the middle of winter.
Sigh with me when crimson petals fade
and shrivel to cocoons of promise.

Pause in the realization that
we too wane on a gentle slope,
sliding toward being absolutely nothing.
Enjoy the personal moment of melancholy.

It is the realization of the need for
a new perspective – of an urgent need
to remain valid although still on
that slope of becoming irrelevant.

We are each going to vanish from life.
Find and attach yourself to a positive dream.
Cast aside seeking entry to a hereafter where
you can affect nothing. Do good things now.

2013

JUST A SWOON

Suzanne, when life tosses me aside
like a stone into the bottomless pond
I hope you can count my silence as just a
swoon, not a light forever extinguished.

The junipers we watched will still sway
as icons of the beauty we shared
And what of the night stars and clouds?
There, did you see that bright star set?

I hope at least one of my poems
keeps you in warm comfort
as you have kept me throughout
our loving lives together.

2019 Prescott

MAN WITHOUT A GUN

A while back I pensioned my guns.
collected over 55 years. They were
friends I hunted with when younger,
full of oats and mistook hunting
for manhood. I liked their feel and
smell and the back-of-mind notion
that I could defend family and home.

I sold them to an old friend and
collector of historic small-bore rifles.
Long-lens cameras are my hunting tools now
– more satisfying, and nothing dies.
He has made the same conversion.

At 73 years, I realize no one is interested
in molesting me, and anyway, I can only shoot
one gun at a time. I keep one revolver Dad
handed down in case I need to dispatch
coyotes eying my sheep or poultry.
In truth l'd never use a gun against
a human unless it's a gun-toting coward
threatening unarmed civilians, if I had a gun
on me at the time, which is unlikely
and if the shooter was a berserker,
which is all too likely these days. . .

2014

THE CHALLENGE

The promises of free enterprise
are profound, yet rely heavily
on population growth because
bigger is always better — isn't it?

Yet massive population growth
mothers poverty, malnutrition, famine,
pollution, resource depletion, war
climate change and nature's retreat.

Can capitalism invent prosperity
not dependent on population growth?
Can free enterprise overcome the
calamities of unfair wealth distribution?

Can capitalists moderate their greed
so that its promise is fulfilled for
the many and not just the talented,
the lucky few and the profit driven?

Is greed more powerful
than justice, equality and balance?
It is too often so.

2015

RACE TO PERDITION

A quarter moon slowly arcs through
oceans of stars burning tiny random holes
in our jet black canopy. Each star a diamond
bringing universal messages audible to those
able to commune with galaxies and suns.

Listen closely, hear the roar
of an expanding universe, muffled
by time and distance to vaporous whispers
racing freely in the vacuum of space
despite the restraints of gravity and time.

Galaxies, fiery echoes of their origins,
reveal the unfolding of motiveless energy
spinning into fantastic pinwheels of gravity
racing from timeless ether to massive density
in atomic pulsing lullaby of physics.

Offering no motive for anything's existence
except the laws of physics and the creative forces
of random occurrences within chaos, there comes
an unlikely creation of soft sentient beings capable
of self-change to survive in their environment.

Then come humans breeding faster than war, disease,
aging, pollution or natural calamities can kill them off.
They overwhelm the planet as religion and capitalists
spur population growth for profits and power

while fouling land, air and water – the nasty
by-products of out of control growth.

"More is better" is a lie perpetuated by the elites.
The race to perdition accelerates as poverty swells.

2021

PLANT NURSERIES

Houses of religion remind me of plant nurseries
in early spring — filled with annuals and shrubs,
vibrant, budding or flowering plants and promises
of beautiful futures to gardeners of faith.

Along nursery walls, burlap and plastic bags of
fertilizer, mulch and manure stacked like prayer books
ready to nourish plants and give confidence to believers.
Plastic bottles of green and yellow filled with pesticides
or herbicides stand ready to exorcize weeds and
insects sent by Lucifer to perplex gardeners.

And finally, there by the door
is the well-oiled cash register
ready to make money from it all.

2008

POOR GOD

Some call God a patient listener
with ears open to all prayers
coming his way. This may explain
why God, after giving mankind
freewill, went mad so long ago.

When billions pray to be forgiven,
does God sigh and pour another rum?
Considering the selfish prayers
God has heard, I worry that the
old chap has fallen off the wagon.

2018

JUST LISTEN

Native American music
	American folk music and
	Country western music
	Mexican ranchero music
	or an oboe concerto
transport me to a peaceful inner space —

Each provide relief and mental elbow room
	away from blathering billboards
	the bull horns of TV and the internet
	with their emphasis on redundant
	hatreds and haughty divisive hollering
	of politicians, political parties and preachers.

I wish they would shut up
	and just listen for a change.

2021

SMALL BRAIN BURSTS -
SOME MAY AMUSE

◆ Rough yet softened with age, I think of when
my feathers were fine and bold of color.
Now I push such ruminations aside
for they represent what is both lost and
foolishly enriched with embellishing fancies.

◆ Throughout my life every fresh breeze
brought surprise and love to my eyes
and affection for those who joined me.
How tiresome are those who have lost
the role of starry-eyed romance.

◆ As one ages it is nice to be admired
for more than being a "good patient."

◆ On your journey, catch small moments,
look up from the business / money game.
Enjoy the aura of magnetic people
and the glow of kind "hellos."
Be nice to people who wait tables –
they must be nice to grumpy strangers.

◆ Aging brings two benefits:
The first is perspective. The second is that wrinkles don't hurt.

◆ "The IRS" spells "Theirs."

◆ To be independent is not a license to be offensive.

◆ To recognize what is funny suggests you are sane.
  To see everything as funny suggests you are insane.
  To see nothing as funny just makes you mundane.

◆ The power of venomous verse means little in an age when
  few read poetry. An exception may be the music of Rap.

◆ What God may actually have said was: "My work is done, let
  there be science."

◆ Poems: visible manifestations of an otherwise private
  personal struggle sometimes reduced to metaphor.

THANK YOU LI PO

Summer half-moon above Granite Mountain.
Pleiades scratches the dark enigmatic sky.
At rest thinking of you, I pass into sleep.

The cathedral's stained-glass vaults leak yellow light
onto its marble floor. A bouquet of marigolds.

Roof patio above old city night.
Reduces us to essential elements —
rum, cheese, philosophical talk.
Beyond, lightning above the volcano.

My father's heart became a stunted lemon tree
and its bitter fruit hung out of reach,
surrounded by formidable thorns.

One hundred tourists admire the bantam wren on canyon
ledge below. None toss a bread crumb. Bird is gone.

Owls on hillside call out in a safekeeping way —
beckoning one another.
Their bodies – invisible. Great eyes search.

A summer breeze halts, hides just around the corner,
in unfelt approach and retreat, casting perhaps for words to sigh.

I could never have imagined being so weak,
Parkinsons makes meek my every stair step
where falling might be more than I could bear.

Deer drink from moon where it reflects on pond.
On hard fingertips, crabs clack across wet rocks.

Late afternoon — long shadows of saguaro arms
reach into camp — time for cups of water.

With a cup of wine in moonlight
          my shadow insists it knows me.

2019 Prescott

NEWS OF THE DAY

AP MARCH 22, 2014

Americans own 400 million pets
spend $56 billion a year on them
... everything from special food
to bed-warmers, studded collars,
pet grooming and doctors.

Same page:

Homelessness is epidemic!
No problem — tiny houses,
60, 64, 80 square feet;
mansions at 99 square feet —
built for the homeless
with bed, table, roof;
no water or electricity
and wheels to move them
if neighbors feel threatened.

Page 2

Hate preacher Phelps dies
after lifetime of picketing
funerals of HIV victims.
St. Peter hangs sign
on the pearly gates
"You were no help Phelps –
Go to hell"

2014

NONE BUT THE SIGHTED

His vision began to glaze over
from woman-watching in the plaza –

Such flowers who may see him
as just a smelly old goat.

How many "How dare you!"
glares can a old coot take?

The blind marimba player
paused a moment, thinking

of the fragrant flower a stranger
from the plaza handed him.

2014

THOUGHTS ON NATURE

- A light wind arrives showing no substance in its stealth, yet every leaf and blade of grass swoons in its caress.

- When wind scatters yellow palo verde blossoms upon the sand, can rain be far behind?

- Wind, the essence of liberty, yet must obey the physics of heat and cold.

- Clouds scudding in lacy promise, morph from white to turbulent grey and grow heavy with thunderclaps, heralding what the desert craves.

- Flowers past their triumph yield their form and scent, curl inward in the droop of fulfillment — while ovaries swell in rebirth.

- All stones gain beauty when wet even more interest when polished.

- Thin yellow curtains make bedrooms cheery in the morning.

- Dark feathers of night take flight, scatter high above dawn's downy bosom.

- Spreading great roots to stay erect, the massive Ceiba avoids sinking into rich volcanic earth.

2015

COYOTE SMILES

I wish my coming retirement to be as
            full as the days of my youth —
days when happy hours flew
            by without notice
awaiting only the sunset
            and a campfire meal
after a day of unusual encounters
            and pleasures.

The hours will still pass
            barely noticed
and I have no desire to return
            to the busy business world
where silence is rare,
            deadlines rise like tides
and some eye is ever
            on my work.
I want to live like coyotes —
            they seem ever to smile.

2014

Good Friends

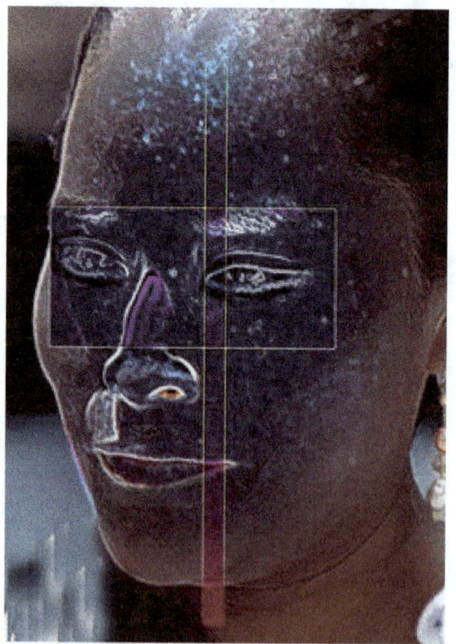

Watching

Easter in Antigua Guatemala: Cucuruchos

Good Friday Procession, Antigua Guatemala

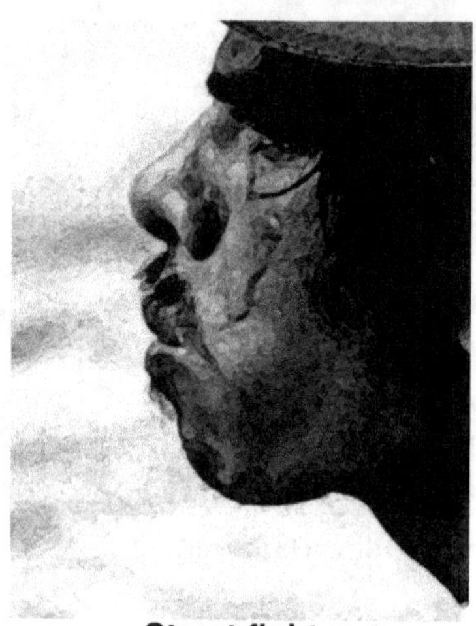

Street fighter

Determination

Guatemala Woman

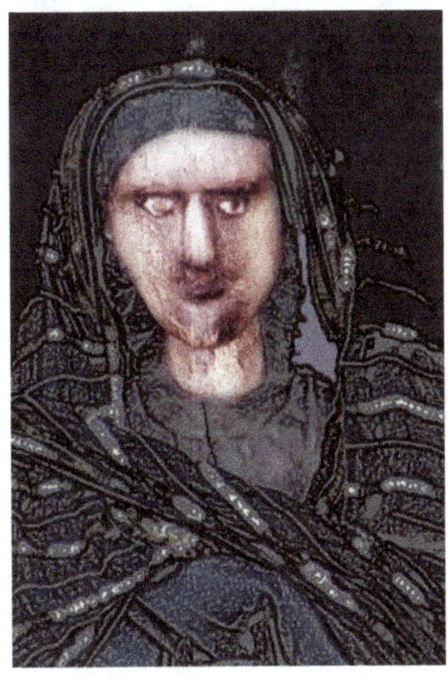

Carved Doorway Saint — Unamused

Creatures, Friends

ON BEES

Fussing and wiggling, determined,
a honeybee disappears into the paunchy
ivory sexiness of a plump yucca flower.

Evident only by vibrating stamen and
low buzzing sounds, it reemerges tired
and dazed, but laden with pollen and nectar.

Stopping briefly to rest, it staggers
and stumbles blindly in the sunlight,
nearly tumbling from the silky flower.

Now hanging upside down it clutches
a petal, tests its wings and cleans its
eyes before winging back to its queen.

2000 Mexico

DRUNKEN BEES

A polished Chinese proverb asserts:
"Wise bees sip not from fallen flowers."
The metaphor is clear enough
but it might be added that other bees
drink juice of fallen and fermented fruit
until they are too happy to fly.

1997 Guatemala

A TREE LIZARD

Who is making that ghostly rustling
beneath fallen pecan leaves?
In a dash a tiny lithe lizard sprints
from leafy cover across scorching sand,
then pauses to look around. You'd think
his belly would fry like a salmon steak.

But by raising on his four legs he puts air
space twixt his soft blue belly and the hot sand
upon which he stands. When his toes get
really hot, he races to and up the tree trunk.

Alert and agile, this hunter of insects shows
little fear. He is hunter, not a ghost. Ask any
house fly or wandering ant if they are quicker
than a blue belly lizard's flashing tongue.

Motionless on the tree's cooler trunk
he is like a fish awaiting a passing meal,
mouth half open — it saves time.
"Enter my range," he muses, "Please do!"

2012

SPRING LAMBS

April morning — new lambs
race and bound on springy legs
across low dirt hills I made for them.

The unmarred blue sky grows
brighter as sun ascends above trees
that shade pasture's morning side.

Tree shadows spiderweb the ground,
the air is calm, sweet and cool
as seven lambs frolic with abandon.

 I edge closer to watch their joyous games
and tho lento my approach, their spunky
games are stilled by instinctive caution.

They look to moms for a clue:
Is this two-legged beast trustworthy?
Their answer is quickly "NO!"

So away they dash to mother's teats.
When I sit halfway up the hill, one ventures
close to test his pluck — but not too close.

I move not a hair, but try to mimic a ewe's grunt,
but he bounds away as primordial memory tells
him I sound more like a wolf than his mama.

2016

18 DOGS

18 dogs have been my pals, starting with
"Spot," a dalmatian who curled with me
wherever, as a boy, I lay my head down. She
walked me to and from grade school.
On vacations, Spot sat with me in Dad's DeSoto,
her head out the window, ears flapping in the wind.

Now our dogs are less intimate — maybe because
I am less playful, although Rosie flops beside
me when I siesta on the lawn, lying still until she
gets worried that my lack of motion signifies death.
She begins to whimper hoping I will spring back to life.

Chiche, Blackie, HueHue, Rosie, Maya, Tikal, Sik'iss
Klunker, Curley and another Spot, Miela, Heinie,
Charlie, Bruno, Dale, Rocky, Flash and Cheeta.
All "pound found." Each morphed from the digging,
chewing and licking everything youthful phase
to the berserk barking watchdog stage, next
to day-dreaming dog watching the world stage
and finally — to the lazy mellow years of
mature adult in serious need of petting.

All our dogs passed through a kaleidoscopic
dream world of no purpose beyond their stomachs
and noses and fannies in need of sniffing;
well, those and barking at luffing tree shadows.

Pet dog perspectives of life's essentials are utopian.
As my saddle-maker brother says when someone
shouts "stupid dog" — "If he's so stupid, why are you
the one toting a lunch pail to work every day?"

2005

It is a heavy burden to be thought
a god by tail wagging dogs —
but its rude for our cat to weigh me
as but her indentured servant.

ONLY BUTTERFLIES

Only butterflies ride currents
    in pursuit of wildflowers
        to frame their orchid wings.

Only butterflies in gentle
    winds arouse buds to burst
        in exposés of desire.

Only butterflies fly mutely
    in pursuit of pennants
        holding the ambrosia of life.

Butterflies ignite my days
    with fancy as do meteors
        delight my eyes at night.

2001

WEAVING BY MOONLIGHT

During early evening hours, the bright
light of the rising full moon is mirrored
in ten thousand shimmering cups waltzing
on dark purple waves of the Sea of Cortez.

Inspired by the sparkling array,
indefatigable spiders weave complex
spellbinding snares between cactus paddles
for what might be caught in the morning.

1966

THE BAR-BACK CALICO CAT

The cantina is so heavy with the music
of mariachis, guitars, trumpets and bold
voices singing bawdy songs to a cheerful
crowd well-oiled with tequila, beer, or wine
that the cantina's veteran calico bar-back cat
puts paws over her nicely pointed ears
then leaps out the door to "see ya" cheers.
Gaining a neighbor's roof and a place
where she can be dignified and aloof, she
curls to enjoy a little snooze unmolested.

2021

CYCLONIC FROLICS

Drifting sideways in nearly
imperceptible warm air currents
tiny weightless flying nymphs swirl
in columns of cyclonic frolic above
our warm summer pasture.
Now and again their column dissipates
as a wind gust upsets their sprightly ranks
— then magically reforms as if held
together by unseen gyroscopes.

2006

IF KITTENS

If cats have kittens
and kittens have mittens
shouldn't ewes have woolens
and skunks have little stinkens?
Racoons would, of course,
have racketeerens.

2010

TURTLE FISHERMEN'S SHACK

As quiet as the warm, still air,
the vacant turtle fisherman's shack
roosts on hot sand beside the
ancient, austere lagoon.

As I pass barefoot
in courteous, cautious silence
a sun-bleached curtain
waves a silent artful greeting.

Beyond the shack, a palm frond
covered lean-to shades sea turtles
immobile where they have been
flipped onto their backs —
a catch awaiting an awful demise.

Sun glares through the haze
on sea beasts destined to be soup
and combs for women's hair.
Oh the conspiracies of men!

I keep walking past as waves
loll at my feet and temptation
to set the turtles free pulls
cautiously at my temperament.

1963
Scammon Lagoon, Mexico

GOATHERD'S DONKEY

The goatherd's donkey
is his one-half horsepower
pickup truck, a sure-footed,
trail-tested four-leg-drive critter
with built-in fuel recycling.

Each morning he walks behind
the flock carrying water, tools
and his own fodder. When homeward
bound, his burden is kitchen firewood
and some days, a goat kid that fell ill.

His Eeyore face and droopy eyes
suggest a disposition of obedience.
Erect ears imply attentiveness
and long lashes suggest affection —
but he'll kick you if he can!

He knows the drill and does his job
no faster than a switch demands.
His eyes scan the hills where escaped
friends, now feral, roam free of humans
who waste a donkey's precious time!

In the wild one day, he watched
three feral donkeys enjoying grazing
while on a slow-paced stroll —
one white, two greys, none
with lead ropes to curb their will.

Each feral casually sampling tasty green
plants beneath bushes along their trail.
Healthy and spry, they kept their distance
from his goatherd master, and cast glares
that said: "Don't think about a hackamore –
We're nobody's slave — not ever again!"

1968
Baja California El Norte

ECLECTIC COMPOSER

In an early morning dream I stood tall,
yet apart in my eighth grade school choir —
a clear voice singing high and confidently,
surprised at the smiles I saw below.

Awakening on my desert pillow,
pre-dawn tranquility engulfs me,
eyes fill with the star-packed sky.
What brought that old memory?

I was in military academy when
instructed to stand in for someone.
Afraid, reluctant, then thrilled
at what happened ... oh the sounds!

Desert mockingbird suddenly
commences a bright morning song –
a trilling soliloquy to life and freedom.
Each note new, extemporaneous, rare.

Feathery nomad of silken scales,
an eclectic composer singing bits of
all the songs he has ever heard,
Is that from a jazz riff I whistled yesterday?

1964

EWES CAN'T COUNT

Lamb triplets — a shepherd's boon?
'Tis not so, for ewes so easily confuse.
Few can count beyond two wiggly tails
so the runt is, sad to say, ignored by mom
or the stronger two take all the milk
and starve the bawling third.

Lambs in twos, is darned good news.
Lambs in threes, no thank you please!

2003

BE COYOTE

Oh to be coyote on a hillside —
      reposing beneath mesquite.
Blameless gazer watching
      for my next meal.

Minding my own business,
      loping my world
demanding little, satisfying
      all that I require,
no long term plans
      of any kind.

2003

THE LIVES OF TWO DOGS

Feral City Dogs

Antigua, the old colonial city, harbors hundreds of feral dogs,
all skin on bone, foraging for scraps amidst shuffling tourists
and shopkeepers who shoo them from shaded doorways.

Limping on dislocated hips earned in dog fights or store-owner
kicks, one can see they are sick in body, feel unwanted and
afraid, wondering — *will I ever have a friend?*

What is a fleabag to do? None will feed or pet you.
Few offer even a friendly word, and competitors for food
include other desperate dogs, poor people and even grackles.
Your mama is gone, probably dead. Every day is a fight
for edible garbage and at night warm dry place to sleep
is hard to find, for it rains a lot in Antigua.

Family City Dog

Around a fire pit, star-watching, talking sometimes,
        more often sitting mesmerized by the coals,
                marrow bones given to each dog.

The smallest pooch lies under my chair
        his bone between his paws hoping
                to avoid thievery by the bigger dogs.

Their gnawing chorus brings laughter
    until jaw tired, they settle down to nap,
        the bigger ones seek a petting hand on head
           the small ones beg for a comfortable lap.

Before long, we are all peacefully asleep.

2011

COLONIAL CAT BYWAYS

For a decade or two we owned a graceful
      colonial home in Antigua.
It was stylish with arched doorways
      flowers, patios,
fireplaces and thick adobe walls
      that Spaniard "conquerors"
left behind after the great earthquake
      shook Guatemala.

Once a bustling monastery
      floored in stone and red tile,
its tall rammed-earth walls still
      stand as they were intended
– barriers to the outside world
      of poor and uneducated society –
part of a Spaniard legacy that endures.

But the tops of its 8-foot walls
      have become roads for feral cats
to slink to and from neighborhood homes
      small cafes, bakeries and kitchens
in search of mice and cockroaches.

The monastery failed long ago so now
      there only remain renovated rooms and
exterior walls onto which sunlight thrills
      vines of passion fruit, morning glories,
raspberry vines and bougainvillea
      to brighten the courtyards and fountains.

Citrus trees have grown to copse.
          A stone footpath leads to our vegetable garden.
At night the yard is alight with random
          beacons of fireflies and the swift motions of bats
hunting among persimmon and coffee plants.

2013
Antigua

SMALL WONDERS

No light house warns
captains, go cautious in the night.
            No sandcastles
                        face a melting tide.
There is nothing here but
            what nature lays down,
                        no explanation.
                                    Just itself.

Chipmunk sentinel on rock ledge
contemplates waves below —
        or something beyond
                    the limits of time.
He turns to survey
        the desert hills behind,
                    but nothing unnerves, so
                                he resumes munching seeds.

Standing in a philandering wind,
        does he wonder how many
                    small wonders there are like him.

2014 Peru

RAYA AT 20

With age, our cat Raya became
the epitome of indignant royalty
coupled with dignified carriage
and restrained curiosity
so characteristic of elderly house cats.
When she deigns to let us pet her head
while sitting sphinx-like and looking
stoically away, a twitch in her tail
betrays a faint purr of indolent pleasure.

2004

SONORAN LIZARDS

Sonoran lizards —
welcome consumers of flies and ants
yet lizards seem so vulnerable and naked
surrounded by larger beasts that cleave and tear
with fang or claw or beak, in the rude belief that
lizards look ever so much like lunch meat.
If lizards weren't so doggone fast
would they join reptiles of the past?

2017

WHEN I BECAME A LIZARD

I have no memory of when or why
I became a lizard
but I found myself flat-bellied
on sunning rocks
doing pushups while eying
the ground for tasty ants
of the right size and retardation.

It's a quiet life.

2018

ON THE CRAB

Grown hard on his back side
his legs add little beauty.
Walking in sideways scurry,
his beady eyes search
for carrion with claw primed
to swivel, rend and tear.
To others in his salty world
his approach must be arresting.
How can such a repulsive fellow
make such a succulent dish?

1962

TWO TRAILS

Ankle deep on loose sand
in dunes of flawless geometry
I pursue survival that lies

beyond the immense poverty
of a dune range I must
escape or die within.

On a slope I am stayed by
nearly imperceptible tiny
tracks cross my path –

something recently alive,
that seems to have come
from and gone to nowhere.

A beetle with long legs lifting
its body above the hot sand?
Did it land, hunt – then fly away?

Perhaps it lives below the surface,
emerging to attack a fussing stray ant
then digging itself away from the sun.

Here and there pygmy avalanches
made by its tiny feet erase its trail.
No signs of combat can be seen.

Gently I touch its footprint.
A new conical landslide appears
beneath my finger – then expires .

Rising, I look at my own trail
ending in the depression where I
I paused to touch an unknown.

2011
Sand dune range north of San Felipe

HUEHUE, OUR CATTLE DOG

In the tedious periods between meals
only one of our five farm dogs pays serious
attention to our existence – Huehue,
a cattle dog we rescued from the county pound.

When new he ran away twice until a light
dawned that meals we provide are regular,
and free of ants, gravel or bits of stick.
And marrow bones appeared almost weekly.

Other realizations sealed the deal:
he has the run of the farm, petting is
not absent-minded, baths are optional
and thick grass facilitates snoozing.

Huehue views the other dogs as useful
when he wants to play ... but hopelessly stupid.
He does not bark at phantoms or the moon —
but no stranger enters without his permission.

2011

DOGS WHO KNEW US

Dogs who knew us are buried
in our desert arboretum where
coyotes cannot disturb their sleep.

In their honor we plant blue acacias
that blossom yellow each spring and
whose bark howls blues to the moon.

Their names are still loved and whispered:
Quiche, Klunker, Charlie, Huehue,
Heinie, Zuni, Spot, Bippie and little Flash.

2003

PLEASANT COMPANY

Butterflies flitting in broken light
pass beneath palo verde's
flowering yellow canopy.

Each outrageous in its colors
both pleasant, silent company
and genteel as summer clouds.

2010

CRICKETS

What creature is purer of heart
on a calm warm summer night
than the bantam brown cricket?

It seems not bothered to be a
tiny and a tempting morsel
to birds, lizards, scorpions or cats.

Each sings throughout the night
asking for no more than warmth
to set its metronome a-ticking.

2004

TO BE A HONEY BEE

If they lived a good deal longer than they do
I'd fancy being a honey bee for a day or two
zooming to happily hover and thrum above
a hillside perfumed by new wildflowers.

Their rainbow glow in amber sunrise
drawing me to hover close above
and with my compound eyes admire colors
in spectrums none but bees can see.

Without delay I would light gently amid
their sunlit glow, that I might enjoy their passion —
then submerge myself within, collecting pollen
as my honey tongue sucks sweet nectar.

With pollen-loaded hair I'd diddle other blooms
 – then fly to my queen's hive where
in ecstacy I would dance among my brothers
and boast of where I found such honey pots.

2021

QUAIL

1.

It is plain to see from the nature of quail
           that they cannot live alone.
Each day they bob and dash about
           seeking to find their own
Hearts of quail must not be kept apart.

2.

Sitting nervous atop pasture fence
a bobwhite quail cries unrestrained:
"Where are y'all? I am all alone!
Where are y'all?" I am so alone!"

Close by, yet beyond a golf course
hedge, her family bevy calls back,
"We're here, over here!"
Hurling herself into the air with a startling
buzz of wing strokes, she pumps, glides,
alights and in bobbing dash disappears.

Beneath a tree I sit apart, content among flowers
and piped music, not at all lonely, for my home
is where I am and my love is here too.

3.

Blistering day ends its cycle.
Quail in bevy dart about the brush,
under fences, on walls, scurrying on
paths free of dogs, cats or joggers.

Heading to secret roosts, their calls
so plaintive, meek and so frightened,
I feel ashamed to find their precarious
trek home humorous to watch and hear.

Sunshine fades, mountains turn blue
shadows to purpled black. Their cries cease.
Do they roost safely, their little hearts slowed
to evening's calmer more loving rhythms?

1989 - 2001

NAPPING NELLY

Certain the world was designed for stalking, cats
chase to kill crickets, mice, rats – even cockroaches.
Tabbies, whom we all like to passively watch
ever jump, stalk and play "my tail to catch."

Nelly, our calm old yellow-eyed feline weighs with
disdain my "come kitty" calls as puny reason to rise,
and signals with a yawn, that my offer of petting her gently
on my lap has already disturbed her comfy nap.

Lying half awake on the window sill
she sees a wren or two she'd like to catch.
So engrossed, her ears now twitching
has she forgotten her jowls might need scratching?

But the calmness of her yellow eyes
says she'll stay just where she lies
– there will be no moving from the sun
where her first morning nap has just begun.

2013

WING SHADOWS

Backlit against the pale blue summer
morning sky, a red-tailed hawk circles
slowly in its practiced, patient style of hunting.
Its shadow briefly sweeps across my path,
reminding me of its imperative to appease
hunger by catching and consuming
small game that linger outside their
cozy burrows too long after dawn,

To the hawk, I am an irrelevant curiosity.
Its interest is on much smaller fare which
even from a great height, his powerful
vision enables him to spot and target.
Pity the rabbit who thinks himself safe
among the cactus but blinks, and misses
the hawk's bullet-like dive from above..

After hunting most of the night, a bull snake
lies somnolent and content in the warming
morning sun, digesting a plump pack-rat.
Suddenly from out of the tranquil sky, the hawk
appears, its talons and beak quickly doing their work.
For the snake, life ends in a flash while
for the hawk, the catch is two meals in one,
but a meal it finds a little difficult to carry back
to his fledglings – it is heavy and continues
to writhe in the throes of death.

1970

EACH NOTE EXACTLY
WHAT SHOULD FOLLOW

As dawn transforms our acres,
a desert bird, half awake, unsure,
            offers a few odd notes,
            as it tunes up.

Then — silence.

It makes a second effort,
            more like a song,
            but still loosely cobbled.

Another silence until its symphony
of self-recognition, territoriality and joy
breaks forth to command all ears with,
as Bernstein said of Beethoven,
            each note,
            exactly what
            should follow
            its predecessor.

EVdB 2012

KILLDEER

Killdeer in their splendid epaulettes
offer clear voiced in-flight outbursts
declaring their worldly bearing —

then aground, hunt daintily
on a freshly irrigated field
for insect delicacies.

Still vocal at night above our fields
declaring their well-fed presence
and contentment to be invisible.

2010

PELICANS & SEA GULLS

Pelicans strike me as wise old-world
philosophers without portfolio and reluctant
to push their world views of a Buddhist sort.
Maybe they have learned that privatizing
their views avoids the risk of violence
— an additional hallmark of their wisdom.

But having never heard a pelican speak, sing
or even squawk, I speculated that by nature
they might be hermits – but that can't be right,
they daily fly together in "V" or "L" formations.

Then there are sea gulls: their smooth heads
containing a food gauge, always pointing to "empty."
A gull's appetite is driven by brain lobes
demanding they quarrel, snatch food and flee.
In their world of grizzly pickings, manners and sharing
are at the far margins of motive. I once saw a gull
pause, briefly, before seizing a glob of rotting jelly fish,
then dashing down the beach before his brethren
could steal some of it from him.

Yet gulls have some admirable attributes:
They can float and soar serenely on nearly any
wind or wave the sea offers when tempestuous.
They routinely decorate drab coastal rocks with icing
And gulls entertain with a haunting sentimental caw —
"Why oh why am I always so hungry?"

1964

SEA BREEZE MASTERS

On motionless wings, playmates of wind
expose the currents to earth-bound creatures.
Soaring and swooping like gliders,
they fill the mist with white motion and
muffled cries – "we are wind masters!"

Now a rising gale makes wild the sky,
driving the wind sculptors from their princely
aerial games and weightless flamboyance
to vulgar flat-footed perches where, hunkered down
on the sand, they stand like miniature gargoyles,
each facing into the wind, alone and resigned.

1964

NOTHING MORE ELEGANT

This day offers nothing more elegant
than the beauty of virgin mountains where
thermal winds lift casting birds of prey
above a vast theater of desert plants
sculpted into shapes elegant and austere.

Night offers silent desert renewal
as nature's aromas on cooling breezes
delight all things now free of day's heat.
Moonlight becomes the long-awaited
garment of tranquillity and repose.

2001

SONGS OF JOY

Ever ready to assail encroachers
with swoops, trills and rasps,
the mockingbird marks
the frontiers of her territory,
hostile toward anyone who questions
her thoughts about safety and space.

Then nightly she sings of joy
and perhaps to a mate of love.
She is a composer who sings for joy
and she brings the same to me.

2001

MOCKINGBIRD'S DELIGHT

Burst open like over-ripe watermelons,
their ruby-red pulp bejewelled with shiny
black seeds ripening in Sonoran sun,
saguaro fruit beckons a mockingbird.

Being first to spot the treasure, she quickly
and haughtily lands on the saguaro's spiny
crown, oblivious to cactus defenses, for now
the rich moist fruit is hers alone.

Willing prisoner to her joyous triumph
she gives brief voice to a blustery song.
She did not land there merely to brag,
but to fill her belly and enjoy the sweet juice.
Soon she is busy prying free her breakfast.

Casting aside fruit skin, some seeds fall
to applauding pack rats below. She lifts both
wings to show her delight for such refreshment —
but cocks her head to check for hawks above.

2016

FIDDLER CRABS IN SCAMMON'S MARSH

Hundreds scurrying, their bellies on
wet marsh sand cast no shadows
but when amassed in legion, move
like low-flying magic carpets.

Arrogant fiddler crabs assemble
in ranks, blanketing the muddy sand,
each a warrior — collectively an army of claws
and beady eyes, yet conservative bravado.

Between muted waves of the salt marsh
they advance, halt, stand their ground
then quickly retreat in some strategic
purpose that is perplexing to me.

Like swarms of defiant midget Vikings,
each hefts a big claw geared for pillage
and each is ready for a bash
if opportunity provides a path.

But perhaps their claws are really banjos
and they are wandering minstrels
heading to a seaside fiddler's slam,
but I hear no music, not a single note.

Though my advance is slow I must appear
gigantic – all but two break ranks to scurry
and hide in sandy holes or into the forest
of salt water reeds from which they ventured.

But two, probably crabby colonels, stand
apart, firm, with claws raised, contemptuous —
until my advance and towering size convinces
both to retreat and fight another day.

2011

TIRED LEGS

Two bundles of firewood
        weigh on his back,
sag his old belly toward
        the parched ground.
The hard loads rub and grate
        against his calloused sides,
making pains only donkey
        nerves can feel.
Tired in his legs, he walks
        the worn desert trail
on sand ground into powder
        from so many earlier trips.
Moving no faster than he must,
        counting his hoof marks
from the morning outbound trip
        he bears firewood and kindling
that will never warm his nights.

1978
Queen's Well, Az

TO THE COTTONTAIL

Short-eared as rabbits go
yet brave, to live where hawks,
coyotes, bull and rattle snakes
prowl with bunnies on their minds.

Swift little critter with innocent eyes
and powder puff tail, too bad your
taste and size oft lead to your demise.
Were I you, I'd hide in warrens too.

Ever munching tender-tufted grass
with dainty manners, your only fault
is leaving poop everywhere behind,
as you seek a shady hill on which to recline.

2015

RABBIT IN CAMP

Cottontail pauses beneath creosote
bush near camp, then hops cautiously
to a cluster of golden dry seed-tufted grass.

I move no muscle that might frighten the brave
little critter. As much as me, he deserves a tranquil
breakfast nibbling on sweet wild wheat seeds.

Closer he edges to where I sit and must
feel safe, for he settles on his haunches,
paws uplifted and chews in his bantam way.

When sated, he lies down with ears pressed
close against his body and appears just an
odd-shaped stone a hawk might overlook.

2015

TWITCHING

Above on a jumble of stately boulders
a twitching motion catches my eye,
then is gone — I freeze – wait.

A small grey animal rises to peek
at what I am, another head emerges
then both duck to discuss the matter.

Might I resemble some grave peril
to be weighed against their need
to hunt for seeds and leaves to eat.

The desert rock squirrels peek again
then fully emerge, forepaws curled
as they haunch-sit and watch me closely.

Both tails twitch again, then again.
One looks left, the other right –
I scratch my nose and both are gone.

2015

WE PUT KIND OLD
HUEHUE DOWN TODAY

Kindness is learned in the school of pain
where presumptions of the future turn ashen
when a loved one cannot tell you what is wrong,
as he loses control of everything.

Reality creeps cruelly from the dark as the future
dissolves before your eyes, slowly, inescapably,
and painfully like an oozing wound. I must make a
decision that kills a helpless friend and weakens me.

Memories of his gentle personality flow,
but with the injection he goes to a desolation,
as I am homebound in a truck where he used
to stare out the window in amazement
as wind flapped his ears and teared his eyes.
Now it is my eyes that weep.

One learns the gravity of friendship in a world
where "gotcha" is our modern credo but
he was one who journeyed through
each night with our safety in mind.

Only kindness makes sense anymore,
only the kindness where we help
each other through the day
and where kindness whispers:

It is I you have been looking for
and I will walk with you as a friend.

2016
On the death of Huehue, a cattle dog we rescued from the
pound some 15 years before.

NOT ALWAYS MIST

There are billions of birds
everywhere, all of the time.
Mostly above us —
sitting, pecking, flying, arguing
singing, floating on thermals
primping, even cooing and billing,
and pooping with such regularity
that you must remember, it is
not always mist you feel
on your forehead.

2008

PELICANS – THEY ARE AIR ITSELF

A brown pelican with something broken
limps weakly, pitifully on wet sand,
struggling to stay upright, but unable
as small waves sweep his exhausted body
out of control, scotching his frantic efforts
to evade my curious advance.

In my hands, this master of wave-top gliding
looks dully at me, pathetic, suddenly resigned,
anticipating sudden death from this huge predator.
I now understand how pelicans can fly, glide
and cruise above waves so effortlessly:
they weigh nothing at all — they are air itself!

My curiosity turns to compassion as I feel his broken
wing and in camp splint it with tape, feed him water,
bits of fish, warm his ebbing spirit by the fire.
We watch one another until sleep demands its due.
Dead in the foggy morning, I set him on a dune
where scavengers will make new life from his remains.

1964 Mexico

PELICANS

Perpetually cool and restrained
pelicans know they are cool artists,
and feel free to lead their shadows
skimming above pulsing waves —
making undulating art of level flight.

2009 Guatemala

DEER GHOSTS

Dawn has barely lifted her skirts
as ground fog fashions the forest blue.
A small family of does and fawns
rise steaming from their leafy beds,
floating ghostly through the fog.

2020

MULE DEER AT SUNRISE

Fades now the purple hour, turning from gold and
red to silver, until rising sunlight floods the ground
except where shadowed by pine and oak.

We watched three mule deer bed down last night
and see they suffered only a dusting of snow
'though they hoped to sleep protected under a thick
canopy of our ancient alligator pine trees.

The mule deer rise from warm pine needle beds,
stretch and check that their cold stiff legs
will hold them steady when they begin to forage.
Hind legs reach forward to scratch nuisance itches.
With graceful balance each shakes snow from hips
and shoulders, takes a few steps, intent to search
for leaves and nuts that linger in the forest.

We two watch through our bedroom window
sipping warm tea and nibbling on oatmeal cookies.
They ignore us, but their ears and noses are alert
for scent or sounds of a pair of large coyotes
known to hunt the trails in this forested neighborhood.

2022

MISSING ALL SUMMER

In such heat, newcomers might
not detect summer edging
toward autumn, but in the infinite
spaces beyond cognition, I sense
humble changes in air and plants
— a murmur hailing gentler climes.

Dawn hours speak most clearly as I
crawl from my bedroll and nature
informs skin how much cooler it can be
at night as the sun eases south
and air temps shun the century mark.
Cactus flowers number fewer.

Deciduous mesquite and ironwood trees
slowly sprinkle their tiny leaves onto
thickening mats below. Ants scurry
with burdens to stock the queen's nest.
Now come the songs of orioles
and cardinals I missed all summer.

2016

FALLEN FLEDGLING

Fallen to earth, a tiny fledgling
      with too few feathers to fly,
lies dusty, weak, panting ...
      has it no chance?

If our cat or dog overlook her
      ants will eat her alive,
one is already on her head,
      glaring into her confused eye.

I brush away the opportunist,
      cup the infant in warm hands,
and search the pecan tree for its nest
      — but see nothing.

No escape does she try to make
      so helpless – I cry.
She sees nothing, trembles in throes
      of fear and weakness.

Drops of water on her beak seem welcome
      — did she really swallow?
Her eyes open and close. Is she eyeing
      me with hope or fear?

Do my warm hands give her incentive?
      Did the water revive her a little?
Unsure what to do I sit with her –
      but then her eyes close for good.

Water on her open beak goes nowhere.
       Slowly her tiny head slumps forward,
is stilled, then flops to one side.
       Her little life is gone.

Saddened, I place her corpse on an
       ant hill for nature's recycling.

2008

CLOCKWORK ANT

In preposterous stagger, a black ant
struggles doggedly to master a forest
of sticks, plant debris, grass and pebbles
as he follows a pheromone trail only
ants can sense to find their way home.

His six legs churn in resolute purpose
until suddenly a desert mule deer trots past –
its hooves heave asunder the ant's world
as might a tornado that drops from the sky –
then disappears, its terrible work done.

Yet the pheromone trail is rediscovered
and followed until at his queen's nest
the little fellow and the seed he carries
disappear. He deposits his tiny burden,
receives instructions and departs to his next load.

The black ant's city cousins enjoy flatter trails
and work together in amazing ways,
in unison, hefting heavy food trophies
and dragging them back to mama's nest

2009

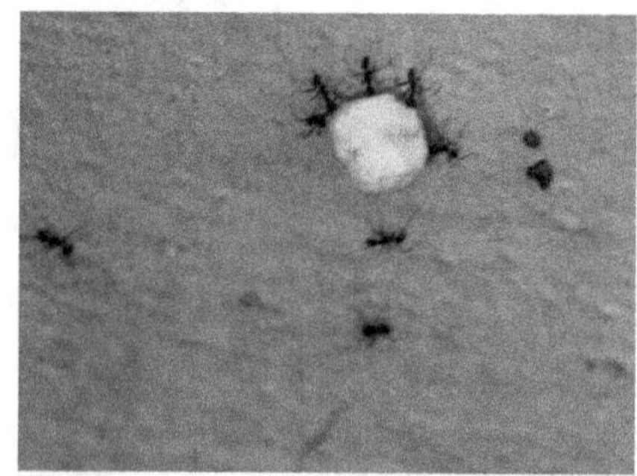

AMONG MARSH REEDS

So alone in blue-grey fog
among emerald marsh reeds,
a single white crane stands
beckoning with arching cry
for its wayward mate
to answer and return.

1995

SEARCHING AT DUSK

A mourning dove, weary from
foraging for earth-fallen seeds
while eluding raptors and cats,
circles a pecan tree in the failing light
of dusk, searching for a safe roost

More instinctive than cognitive,
she must land quickly or risk bashing
into something. Faced with several
poor choices that could destroy
her, she finally flutters safely to one.

High in winter's naked pecan tree,
she regrets the teeter-totter branch
she chose and hops to one less
likely to upset her stomach in a wind
or break away as she sleeps.

2004

OUR YOUNG CAT

Our young tabby rises from sleep
                with a great yawn,
displaying dazzling teeth, pink tongue,
                her arched spring-loaded spine,
and gazes around her kingdom.

After stretches, she cleans her paws,
                checks the sky and sun
to get the time of day,
                concludes the feeding hour
has not yet arrived.

So she cleans her paws once more
                jumps gracefully from her chair
and then ambles away
                search of careless crickets
in the garden, or with luck, a mouse.

2002

SCAVENGERS

Lithe black and dun grackles
        strut in gleaming feathers
saucily, royally, irreverently
        around splashing waters
of the mermaid fountain, incessantly
        quarreling and screeching at
park pigeons who dare claim rights
        to tossed breadcrumbs.

Their piercing voices vex not
        the cooing pigeons
for what sky rats lack in size they
        redress with numbers and agility.
Then surprise ... when food is at issue
        mourning doves arrive with
disrespect for royalty, pigeons
        and any pretense of rules.

Ignoring all three, a oafish hobo
        in dirty rags and torn hat
tips park garbage barrels,
        peers analytically inside
before sorting for discarded
        food and drinks.
Being of like feather, he casts an
        old cupcake to the birds
and stands back to watch the fight.

2016 Antigua

COCKROACHES CHEER US ON

When cockroaches are just a few weeks
             old, they are ready to scurry into
kitchens, bathrooms, pantries, on to buses,
             airplanes, cruise ships, restaurants
and into cafes, ever pleased to panic folks
             enjoying elegant or humble meals.

For eons cockroaches
             think themselves in heaven
as man increasingly proffers
             garbage in every corner
of the planet in tonnage suitable
             to feed roaches for an eternity.

There is no foot-dragging
             within cockroach ranks
even in perilous public places,
             where heavy boots abound.
Their covert plan is to be
             the last life swaggering
on a planet polluted by "civilization."

Doubt they are cheering us on?
             Lift any alley garbage can!

2014

MINDLESS BARKING

There are times when an old dog
        simply must submit
to its primordial urges —
        barking mindlessly at
an unfamiliar shadow
        in the night
a sound on the other side
        of the fence or at
a formless something lingering
        in its memory
— that skittish part of its brain
        unwilling to give it up —
until a familiar voice
        shouts "shut up!"

The trance fades,
        barking trails off
as old dog regains
        dim awareness
that it is standing facing a wall,
        its legs are asleep
and its throat is demanding
        a drink of water.

2011

SOUP BONES

On a flawless spring evening
in weather to be enjoyed half-naked
we retire to the outside hearth.
A low fire for light entertains
and spawns hypnotic pauses.

Earlier I bought marrow bones
for each dog — labeled "soup bones" –
perhaps because so labeled the butcher
gets a better price than for "dog bones."

The butcher, a dog fancier herself
cut femurs so large that our smallest dog
is challenged in every way. We laugh
when the chihuahua's rear feet rise off
the ground as she tries to lift one in her jaws.

A daze fills the eyes of our waggers
as I pass out the fatty delights. One
looks up as if I were a god, reminding me
of how I saw my dad when he took me on
a ferris wheel ride at a county fair.

As realization of their prosperity sets in,
each slips away, collapses on the grass
and begins to worship — holding their treat
between paws, gnawing and licking
each end for the marrow.

Watching the four reverently addressing
their bones, pausing not even once to cast
an appreciative glance in my direction,
I wonder what doggie dreams will follow.

2004

DOG DILEMMA

Noble moon is colossal tonight,
serenely cruising closer than usual
above our pasture and hills beyond.
She seems perfectly content to float
as might a giant pearl in carefree flight.

My dog watches with one eye as
the rabbit in the moon passes close
mocking his inability to jump
high enough to give chase, and
so begins a low mournful howl.

12/1/16

THE MOMENT SHE LOVES

Atop a towering cactus sits a red tail hawk,
her talons numb to the thorny crown.

She waits, listens and watches for motion
to focus her eyes on opportunity below.

Marking out-of-place colors or movement
she quietly turns her head, body and talons

in a little dance to be ready for when she will
switch senses in the moment she loves best

— the moment prey is sighted, surveying stops,
and she launches – eyes target-focused,

– an alert rabbit grazing will flee if hawk
miscalculates or hawk shadow reaches it too soon.

Hawk's wing wind seems a loud torrent to her
but to the calm rabbit, her approach is inaudible.

Closer, closer, and still it does not flee —
she knows the moment she will win.

Adjusts her flaps, tilts right, too late for it to bolt.
She screeches to freeze the rabbit in fright,

then snags it, bites a vital place, dust swirling,
holds the struggling body down, confirms her grip.

Looks around – pumps her wings to get high and
away from coyote who might savor a hawk/rabbit buffet.

1988

RED-TAILED HAWK

Like a figure skater on clean ice,
a red-tailed hawk crafts ellipses
in the sky, moving laterally under
broken clouds, casting, searching
the desert below for live game.
Steady in her effort, part of her ellipse
disappears briefly behind a mountain,
then reappears further away until
gradually I see only half an ellipse
then but a quarter, an eighth –
and then she is gone completely.
Will she return to check if I have faltered?

2010

BIRD FEEDER

Outside our breakfast window
and watched by many, a large iron
bird feeder dish lies face to the sky
atop a tall stout post.

The feeder's narrow brim rail holds
the grain, veggies and bread we lavish
on the dish from falling to the ground
where our cats would waylay the dove, quail,
curve billed thrashers, grackles and wrens
who flock to the feeder when kestrels
are not seen in the sky or trees.

A green parrot and six lovebirds
visited daily last winter. Cardinals and
orioles drop by and hummingbirds
find nectar in aloe flowers below.

Visitors are mostly dove and quail.
Doves may symbolize peace and gentility,
but often compete in combat and anger.
Gripping the raised steel edge
doves display "I was here first" wings,
charge each other, release ugly
birds sounds and force the weaker off.

Losers flutter ineptly to the ground.
Confusion reigns when large grackles arrive
— although bigger in size, by nature they are
cowardly and give ground even to juvenile quail.

2006. Phoenix

RANCH DOGS

Brave and scruffy ranch dogs,
unaccustomed to light-skinned visitors
who speak and odd and unmusical language
respond with "don't tread on me" voices
when we first approach. But their fears fade
to cautious sniffing after their masters
greet us with handshakes and calm words.

As we talk, one young hound is lost in curiosity
and makes nonchalant contact by cautiously
sitting next to me, sniffing my pant leg and hand.
He then allows my slow-moving hand to pet
his shoulder in a way that says he can sense
I know how to show love to a dog.

1967
Pima Res.

MILKWEED

The flowers of milkweed open
right on time, in bold orange floating
atop broad deep-green leaves.

"Thank goodness" whispers a butterfly,
"another year, another migration –
yet why do our numbers shrink?"

Answers a wise monarch elder
"Too many people and their stink
forewarns we soon may be extinct"

Too soon, I think, for what befalls
the monarch and milkweed may
foretell the human extinction path ...

2021

CLICKS IN THE NIGHT

Black beetles lumber like
petite polished armored cars,
sniffing for the opposite gender
or something tasty to eat.

Crickets huddle in dark damp places
raising a ruckus and hoping scorpions
are deaf and can't see them,
for crickets are rated tasty.

Mosquitos whine in search
of blood or ripe sweet fruit.
A praying mantis stalks almost
anything to slay and devour.

Many things go "click" in the night
as the eerie chapel of insect oratory
triggers shivers in the mind. It's best
not to worry about small night sounds.

Unless they are in your bed.

2010

SPRING FOREST

The forest is in spring sexuality
despite little rainfall, galore are
tree leaf and wildflower buds.
Above trails scented of browsing game,
cloud streams etch pale blue skies.

Ten and four deer search for food
as in my 76th spring I count small gifts:
spotted towhee scratches diligently,
hummingbirds compete for nectar.
Murders of ravens cruise in disdain.

Unwearied in their hunt for success
squirrels scurry in nature's bounty;
winter did not dampen their lust for life.
Immobile, one sits upon a rock quietly
contemplating the world. Mysterious, beautiful.

 Such fauna will be here when I am gone
– all that will be missing is my delight.
 Today I will walk with even lighter steps.

2018